Love Is Forever

JOAN WALSH ANGLUND

Love
Is
Forever

Harcourt Brace & Company

San Diego   New York   London

Also by Joan Walsh Anglund

PEACE IS A CIRCLE OF LOVE
A MOTHER GOOSE BOOK
SPRING IS A NEW BEGINNING
CHRISTMAS IS LOVE
LOVE IS A SPECIAL WAY OF FEELING
IN A PUMPKIN SHELL
A FRIEND IS SOMEONE WHO LIKES YOU
CHRISTMAS IS A TIME OF GIVING
CHILDHOOD IS A TIME OF INNOCENCE
HOW MANY DAYS HAS BABY TO PLAY?
POEMS OF CHILDHOOD

Requests for permission to make copies of any part of the work should
be mailed to: Permissions Department, Harcourt Brace & Company,
6277 Sea Harbor Drive, Orlando, Florida 32887-6777.

Anglund, Joan Walsh.
Love is forever / Joan Walsh Anglund.
p.   cm.
Summary: A poetic celebration of the special qualities of love.
ISBN 0-15-201680-5
1. Love poetry, American. 2. Children's poetry, American.
3. Love—Juvenile poetry. [1. Love—Poetry.
2. American poetry.] I. Title.
PS3551.N47L69 1998
811'.54—dc21   97-14793

C E F D B
Printed in Singapore

For Helen Hyman
and her wonderful family,
with happy memories
of all the years we've shared

Love is everywhere about us. . . .

It is always ours to share.

Love is sweet . . . as a rose.

Love is tender
        . . . as a baby,

    gentle
        . . . as a mother,

    and comforting
            . . . as a lullaby.

Love is also strong . . . as a great sea,

enduring . . . as a high mountain,

and sheltering . . . as a tall tree.

Love joins all hearts as one.

Once Love has touched us,
its joy stays within us . . . always.

Love is constant . . . as a star,

trusting . . . as a prayer,

and kind . . . as a good friend.

Love is the center
      of every dream

. . . and the beginning
      of all our happiness.

Love is forever.